HAL•LEONARD
INSTRUMENTAL
PLAY-ALONG

ALTO SAX

Christmas SONGS

T0117629

CONTENTS

2 All I Want for Christmas Is You
4 The Christmas Waltz
5 Happy Holiday
6 I Wonder as I Wander
7 I'll Be Home for Christmas
8 Let It Snow! Let It Snow! Let It Snow!
9 Mary, Did You Know?
10 The Most Wonderful Time of the Year
11 My Favorite Things
12 Silver Bells
13 This Christmas
14 White Christmas

To access audio visit:
www.halleonard.com/mylibrary

Enter Code
6068-5081-8722-7672

Audio Arrangements by Peter Deneff

ISBN 978-1-4950-2554-9

7777 W. Bluemound Rd. P.O. Box 13819 Milwaukee, WI 53213

For all works contained herein:
Unauthorized copying, arranging, adapting, recording, Internet posting, public performance, or other distribution of the printed or recorded music in this publication is an infringement of copyright. Infringers are liable under the law.

Visit Hal Leonard Online at
www.halleonard.com

ALL I WANT FOR CHRISTMAS IS YOU

ALTO SAX

Words and Music by MARIAH CAREY
and WALTER AFANASIEFF

Copyright © 1994 RYE SONGS, SONY/ATV MUSIC PUBLISHING LLC, TAMAL VISTA MUSIC and WALLYWORLD MUSIC
All Rights for RYE SONGS Controlled and Administered by SONGS OF UNIVERSAL, INC.
All Rights for SONY/ATV MUSIC PUBLISHING LLC, TAMAL VISTA MUSIC and WALLYWORLD MUSIC Administered by
SONY/ATV MUSIC PUBLISHING LLC, 424 Church Street, Suite 1200, Nashville, TN 37219
All Rights Reserved Used by Permission

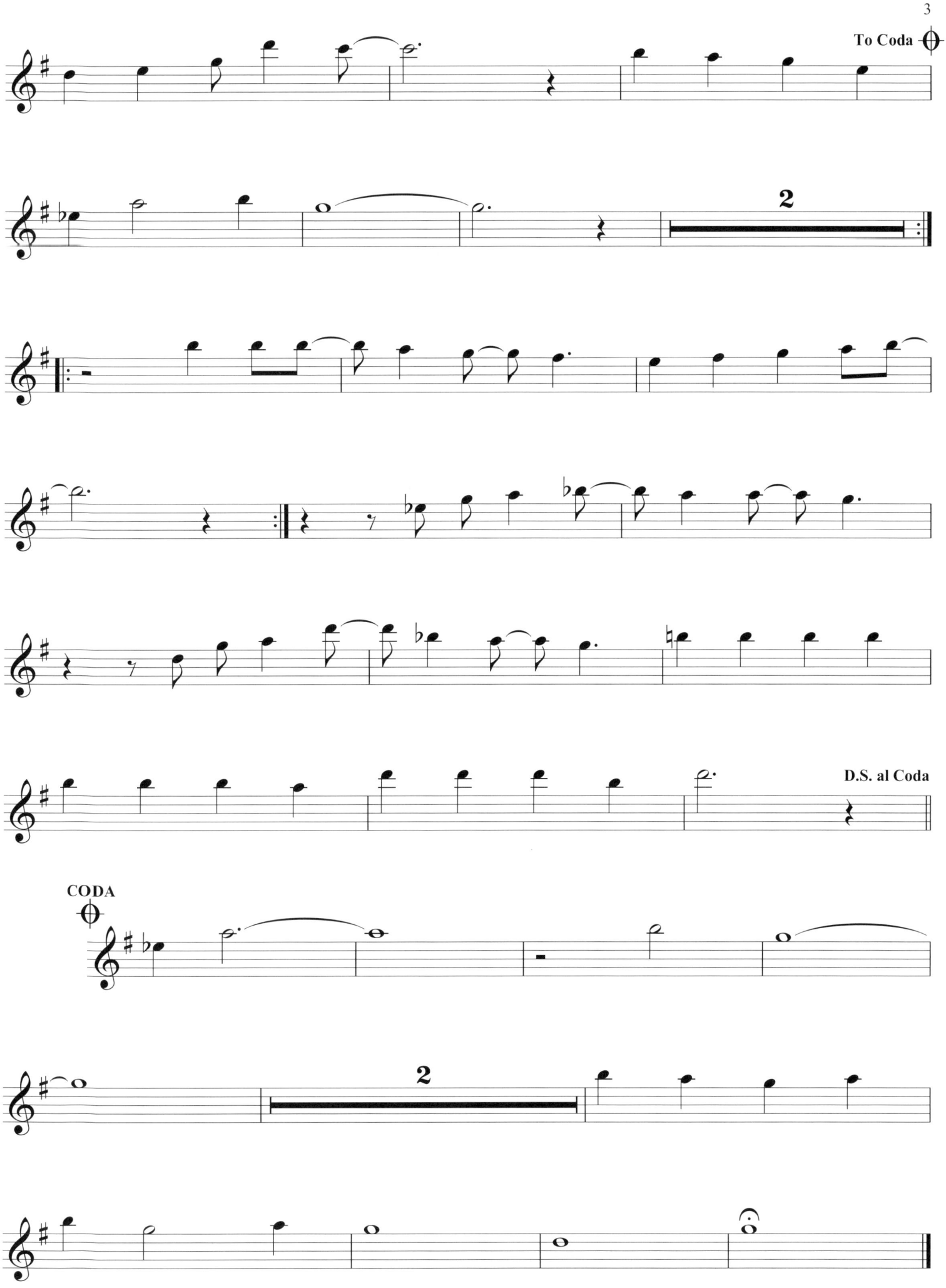
To Coda
2
D.S. al Coda
CODA
2

I WONDER AS I WANDER

ALTO SAX

By JOHN JACOB NILES

Copyright © 1934 (Renewed) by G. Schirmer, Inc. (ASCAP), New York, NY
International Copyright Secured All Rights Reserved
Reprinted by Permission

I'LL BE HOME FOR CHRISTMAS

ALTO SAX

Words and Music by KIM GANNON
and WALTER KENT

© Copyright 1943 by Gannon & Kent Music Co., Inc., Beverly Hills, CA
Copyright Renewed
International Copyright Secured All Rights Reserved

LET IT SNOW! LET IT SNOW! LET IT SNOW!

ALTO SAX

Words by SAMMY CAHN
Music by JULE STYNE

© 1945 (Renewed) PRODUCERS MUSIC PUBLISHING CO., INC. and CAHN MUSIC CO.
All Rights for PRODUCERS MUSIC PUBLISHING CO., INC. Administered by CHAPPELL & CO., INC.
All Rights for CAHN MUSIC CO. Administered by IMAGEM SOUNDS
All Rights Reserved Used by Permisison

MARY, DID YOU KNOW?

ALTO SAX

Words and Music by MARK LOWRY
and BUDDY GREENE

© 1991 Word Music, LLC and Rufus Music (administered at CapitolCMGPublishing.com)
All Rights Reserved Used by Permission

THE MOST WONDERFUL TIME OF THE YEAR

ALTO SAX

Words and Music by EDDIE POLA
and GEORGE WYLE

Copyright © 1963 Barnaby Music Corp.
Copyright Renewed
Administered by Lichelle Music Company
International Copyright Secured All Rights Reserved

MY FAVORITE THINGS

from THE SOUND OF MUSIC

ALTO SAX

Lyrics by OSCAR HAMMERSTEIN II
Music by RICHARD RODGERS

Copyright © 1959 by Richard Rodgers and Oscar Hammerstein II
Copyright Renewed
Williamson Music, a Division of Rodgers & Hammerstein: an Imagem Company, owner of publication and allied rights throughout the world
International Copyright Secured All Rights Reserved

SILVER BELLS

from the Paramount Picture THE LEMON DROP KID

ALTO SAX

Words and Music by JAY LIVINGSTON
and RAY EVANS

Copyright © 1950 Sony/ATV Music Publishing LLC
Copyright Renewed
All Rights Administered by Sony/ATV Music Publishing LLC, 424 Church Street, Suite 1200, Nashville, TN 37219
International Copyright Secured All Rights Reserved

THIS CHRISTMAS

ALTO SAX

Words and Music by DONNY HATHAWAY
and NADINE McKINNOR

Copyright © 1970 by Universal Music - MGB Songs, Kuumba Music Publishing and Crystal Raisin Music
Copyright Renewed
All Rights for Kuumba Music Publishing Administered by Universal Music - MGB Songs
International Copyright Secured All Rights Reserved

WHITE CHRISTMAS

from the Motion Picture Irving Berlin's HOLIDAY INN

ALTO SAX

Words and Music by
IRVING BERLIN

© Copyright 1940, 1942 by Irving Berlin
Copyright Renewed
International Copyright Secured All Rights Reserved

HAL•LEONARD INSTRUMENTAL PLAY-ALONG

Your favorite songs are arranged just for solo instrumentalists with this outstanding series. Each book includes a great full-accompaniment play-along CD so you can sound just like a pro! Check out **www.halleonard.com** to see all the titles available.

Disney Greats

Arabian Nights • Hawaiian Roller Coaster Ride • It's a Small World • Look Through My Eyes • Yo Ho (A Pirate's Life for Me) • and more.

_____00841934 Flute $12.95
_____00841935 Clarinet $12.95
_____00841936 Alto Sax $12.95
_____00841937 Tenor Sax $12.95
_____00841938 Trumpet $12.95
_____00841939 Horn $12.95
_____00841940 Trombone $12.95
_____00841941 Violin $12.95
_____00841942 Viola $12.95
_____00841943 Cello $12.95
_____00842078 Oboe $12.95

Great Themes

Bella's Lullaby • Chariots of Fire • Get Smart • Hawaii Five-O Theme • I Love Lucy • The Odd Couple • Spanish Flea • and more.

_____00842468 Flute $12.99
_____00842469 Clarinet $12.99
_____00842470 Alto Sax $12.99
_____00842471 Tenor Sax $12.99
_____00842472 Trumpet $12.99
_____00842473 Horn $12.99
_____00842474 Trombone $12.99
_____00842475 Violin $12.99
_____00842476 Viola $12.99
_____00842477 Cello $12.99

Coldplay

Clocks • Every Teardrop Is a Waterfall • Fix You • In My Place • Lost! • Paradise • The Scientist • Speed of Sound • Trouble • Violet Hill • Viva La Vida • Yellow.

_____00103337 Flute $12.99
_____00103338 Clarinet $12.99
_____00103339 Alto Sax $12.99
_____00103340 Tenor Sax $12.99
_____00103341 Trumpet $12.99
_____00103342 Horn $12.99
_____00103343 Trombone $12.99
_____00103344 Violin $12.99
_____00103345 Viola $12.99
_____00103346 Cello $12.99

Popular Hits

Breakeven • Fireflies • Halo • Hey, Soul Sister • I Gotta Feeling • I'm Yours • Need You Now • Poker Face • Viva La Vida • You Belong with Me • and more.

_____00842511 Flute $12.99
_____00842512 Clarinet $12.99
_____00842513 Alto Sax $12.99
_____00842514 Tenor Sax $12.99
_____00842515 Trumpet $12.99
_____00842516 Horn $12.99
_____00842517 Trombone $12.99
_____00842518 Violin $12.99
_____00842519 Viola $12.99
_____00842520 Cello $12.99

Lennon & McCartney Favorites

All You Need Is Love • A Hard Day's Night • Here, There and Everywhere • Hey Jude • Let It Be • Nowhere Man • Penny Lane • She Loves You • When I'm Sixty-Four • and more.

_____00842600 Flute $12.99
_____00842601 Clarinet $12.99
_____00842602 Alto Sax $12.99
_____00842603 Tenor Sax $12.99
_____00842604 Trumpet $12.99
_____00842605 Horn $12.99
_____00842606 Trombone $12.99
_____00842607 Violin $12.99
_____00842608 Viola $12.99
_____00842609 Cello $12.99

Women of Pop

Bad Romance • Jar of Hearts • Mean • My Life Would Suck Without You • Our Song • Rolling in the Deep • Single Ladies (Put a Ring on It) • Teenage Dream • and more.

_____00842650 Flute $12.99
_____00842651 Clarinet $12.99
_____00842652 Alto Sax $12.99
_____00842653 Tenor Sax $12.99
_____00842654 Trumpet $12.99
_____00842655 Horn $12.99
_____00842656 Trombone $12.99
_____00842657 Violin $12.99
_____00842658 Viola $12.99
_____00842659 Cello $12.99

Movie Music

And All That Jazz • Come What May • I Am a Man of Constant Sorrow • I Believe I Can Fly • I Walk the Line • Seasons of Love • Theme from *Spider Man* • and more.

_____00842090 Clarinet $10.95
_____00842091 Alto Sax $10.95
_____00842092 Tenor Sax $10.95
_____00842094 Horn $10.95
_____00842095 Trombone $10.95
_____00842096 Violin $10.95
_____00842097 Viola $10.95

TV Favorites

The Addams Family Theme • The Brady Bunch • Green Acres Theme • Happy Days • Johnny's Theme • Linus and Lucy • Theme from the Simpsons • and more.

_____00842079 Flute $10.95
_____00842080 Clarinet $10.95
_____00842081 Alto Sax $10.95
_____00842082 Tenor Sax $10.95
_____00842083 Trumpet $10.95
_____00842084 Horn $10.95
_____00842085 Trombone $10.95
_____00842087 Viola $10.95

Wicked

As Long As You're Mine • Dancing Through Life • Defying Gravity • For Good • I'm Not That Girl • Popular • The Wizard and I • and more.

_____00842236 Flute $11.95
_____00842237 Clarinet $11.95
_____00842238 Alto Saxophone $11.95
_____00842239 Tenor Saxophone $11.95
_____00842240 Trumpet $11.95
_____00842241 Horn $11.95
_____00842242 Trombone $11.95
_____00842243 Violin $11.95
_____00842244 Viola $11.95
_____00842245 Cello $11.95

FOR MORE INFORMATION, SEE YOUR LOCAL MUSIC DEALER, OR WRITE TO:

7777 W. BLUEMOUND RD. P.O. BOX 13819 MILWAUKEE, WI 53213

Prices, contents, and availability subject to change without notice.
Disney characters and artwork © Disney Enterprises, Inc.